Bloom

By: Nashé Wilson

Nashé

Illustrations by

Nashé

&

Aqueyah Brooks

Cover art by

Briah Davis

1

Table of Contents

Chapter II   Between the lines   51

Chapter III   Godspeed   90

Bloom

To Me,
Mami, Destiny, Asia, Kiara, Angelica, Aqueyah,
Roze, Olivia, Taylor, Cheyenne, Sasha, Dre, Tin,
Grammie, Melba, Tewina, Kyrah, JG, Maya, Ash
Kianna, Jalisha, Anthony, Chris, Ari, Fa'aletaua,
Angel, Tommy, Kahlia, Mari, Shanae, Gabe, Gigi,
Cyn, Destiny, Jason, Liv, Taylor, Shadaja, Brenton,
Grandma Betty, Grandma Matty, Ria, Ruhi, Joy

This is my growth

I want you to love boundlessly as if heartbreak is impossible. I want for you to feel so safe in your softness that you give it freely whenever you feel the need. I want you to feel full on days when it's easy to feel empty. To feel carried on days where you can't even crawl. Live like the world is burning, because you owe every day to you.

You know, they say forest fires are good for forests. From the ashes new things bloom.

I

The heartbreak will
Settle onto you in the morning
Do not allow it to glue you
To that bed
The hurt is honest
Get up anyway
It will feel like you can't breathe
But remember
You had lungs
Long before you met them
And you will know breath
For years after they are long gone
They are not a mark against you
Knowing love is a gift
Even following the departure
Of those that we thought
We loved most

Make the Bed

Bloom

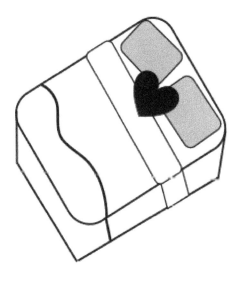

Nashé

There will be
A slipping back
Of things
It's never been
A linear process
The bad showing up
Again is
As human as it comes

As far as life goes

There's one thing I need
To know
Before you go
What would this world be
Without you
Maybe the earth's rotation wouldn't stop
But there will be hearts
That forever skip beats at the sound
Of your name
And birthdays of people you love
Will come and go
And there will always be
An empty chair
Where you should be
There are words you still haven't written
Moments where your heart takes flight
That have yet to come to fruition
Fruits of your long labors
That have yet to sprout
Don't you know
That you are waiting for you
On the other side of all of this
With open arms
And an understanding that you just
Don't have yet
If you go
There may still be light
But it won't be yours
And what failure has beget
Your loved ones
That didn't get the chance to tell you yet

Before You Go

Do not feel
Out of place
On the days when
You move through the world
More like your shadow
Than self
Be assured
You will not blow away
No matter how untethered
You feel
Be still
There is room for that here

Adrift

I allowed
my chest to cave in
To make room
For you

Cave In

Nashé

I so desperately
Wanted to be
The thing that
Loved you out of
Believing
You shouldn't love people

Pray for you

There was a girl
That ventured to
Love the Moon
She waxed lyrical
Of how she smelled of
Sweet air after the storm
Had passed
She is
Just as mysterious
As she seems
Hanging up there
In the celestial
And the deepness of
The navy sky
She carries the same chill
As the night air
And her eyes still shine
Just as brightly
She could tell you stories
Of long starry nights
And right before mornings
Of the riots the Sun makes
As they pass through the sky
She is as fierce as legends
Have told
And what softness you meet
Once you get past the cold
This girl
That ventured to loved the moon
Would stay out all night
If only to see
Her beautiful face
For a second more
To lay in her light
But still

The girl recalled
That morning always came
And the Moon was still
So far away

Light

Bloom

We all want to be needed
Feel it deeply
Want to be necessity
Does that fill you
On the inside
You have always been the middle of a dance
When the music is in full swing
And laughter fills the dance floor
Isn't that forever in just a few seconds
Won't you be there in the morning when the sun comes up
You've transcended light
Been belief for the hopeless
You effectuate prosperity
They have not known any beginnings
But one
You
Be resolved
Demise has no familiarity to you
Vitality lights your steps
And when you walk away
This is catastrophe
You this phenomenon of beings
A blessing to the masses
The night does not beget you
You aren't just a moment
You surely are a memory
Remember these
When you need to be wanted
You aren't finished yet
The music is still playing
And as all the dizzy fades
You have not

Necessity

Nashé

These days I wish we just
Stayed in letters
I so believe that we could have
Been resting between
The lines of ink
At this very moment
I think of the closeness
That could have been stuffed
In those envelopes
What a story line
Pressed between stamps
Pen passageways
That have long since
Gone away
We were just so much better
On paper

Pen Pals

The lonely does bite
After so long
Sitting with it
This snake will make you believe
That the sting
From the venom is sweet
And the lonely has crept up
So slowly
That you grin and bare it
Believe all the bittersweet
Nothing it will eventually leave you with

The lonely

There are days
When being alive
Is all I have to
Give to the world
And that's enough

Softness

Nashé

Oh soft thing
Don't you cry
Those that walked this path
Long before you
Knew
That you were always
Destined to be
So much bigger
Than any of the waves
That would try
To wash you under
As coarse as this
Life that has been handed
To you
Was
Somehow you
Have made
A shiny clean thing
Of it all
You may stumble
Or even trip
But never fall
Don't you worry baby
These thoughts
Are only passing boats
Afterall

Anger begs
Like a discarded lover
Cries in the morning
And refuses to leave
Clutches your sheets
Begs you to stay
Trying to remind you
Of how good you feel
Together

anger

I always just hoped
    That letting go didn't hurt
        As much as the love
            I knew you could never

Give back to me

Unrequited

There are just
So many things that I want
To say to you
So many things that
I had on the tip of my tongue
But so many unused things must
Be useless
They only hold space
That could otherwise be occupied

Could Have Beens

Nashé

You always
        Bit down so hard
                and made the pain
                        So intense

        But somehow
                The fear in your eyes
                        Always convinced me
                                That you were hurting

                                More than I ever was

Hurt people

I wish I didn't write about you
I mean to say
I wish my heart didn't sing
Your praises
Even after a night
Of crying
From sorrows you've wrought
I wish I could look at the moon
And only see the moon and not
You
I wish you weren't the moon

I wish you didn't occupy the
Night sky like you do
Because stars used to be
My favorite
And now I can't lay under them
Without you

I want to see the stars

don't tell me
you need me
it is a lie
that most often leaves the mouths
of lovers who
don't know any better
can't see what the future holds
past the rosy haze that
feelings of affection
can bring

A Lie

you didn't even have
the common courtesy
to leave a note
telling me that you were
all the things you said you'd never be
it feels like the wind has been snatched from
The middle of my chest
No matter how deep my breaths
I cannot inhale

courtesy

Nashé

What is deception
If not a tool
To siphon love
Without
surrendering
one's self

If you ever feel the need
To run
Please do so
As far and as fast
As you need
Even if it means
You're running
Away from me
I know what it is
To be a kept thing
And I have released you
More times than
I can count

But please
Do not run back
Close my door on your way
I no longer desire
To be in waiting
So go quietly
I will clean the mess
Once you leave

Leave

If I'm honest
There is not a single thing
Left in my closet for you
I stopped making room
So please
Leave your bags
At the door
I don't have space
For your things anymore
Pray that make
This space lighter
Equinox coming
It is time for that

Spring Cleaning

In a world
That treats such things
So haphazardly
I know how easy it is
To harden on the outside
When once again
Faced with a wound you spent
Years patching

triggers

Breathe deep
Grief settles in
The lungs
Do not allow it to grow there

Exhale

12/04/19

Bloom

To the love I will be

Once your heart heals from her

Stay soft always

10/18/2020

Somedays
I'm scared
That my words
Have lost their spell
That there
is no longer
magic that intertwined
With my voice
Somehow I must
Have dropped
The poetry from
My speech
On a walk home
That was filled with
The sorrow
Of another
Would be love
That could have
Never made it

TO TOMORROW

I promise it's okay
She tosses herself on the floor
I ask what she needs
She screams
I know that this world
Has made it so she feels the need
To cry until her throat is raw
No more
Baby girl
I will be the barrier between
You
And all that has made you scared to sleep
Ungrit your teeth
Your soft can be open
Here with me
Take your time
I know those big emotions are hard
But I have been building for years
This space is specifically for your tears
No need to worry
You are safe here

Little Love

On any given Sunday
I've been
Damned to hell
Ten times
You see
My brother has OCD
And no matter what
He cannot control
The things that his mind
Has on repeat
And some days
He cannot even see me
Beyond blind rage
And trauma from
Who knows what age
So when I do leave him
I am left to wonder
If that will matter at all
Next to the God he believes in
And the sense of damnation
That never leaves him
I don't have no apologies
Left for who I am
And so maybe
I'll just be damned
I do wonder though
What the penance is
For projecting fears
And how that stacks up
From my little brother
Hurling hell around
As insults all these years
What price do we pay
At the end of life
For all the things we

Never got to say
And all of the things
We never get to

Take back

I can change
I'm willing to work on
I could do
Anything for you
I would give
Anything you asked of me
If you told me to stop
I simply would not breathe
Can't you see this mean squeeze
Tight grip
You got a hold on me
I would have gave you
Everything
it's just
The way I loved
And you
Acted as if
It was less than
Nothing
I can't get that back

Wouldn't breathe

There must be a word
For the grief one experiences
When they've lost
The best parts of themselves
There is no way
To stay unchanged
After making an offering
Of yourself
Only to be turned away

Denied

One day
I'll become the woman
Of your dreams
And then you'll have to wake up
because you already left me
Gone are days
Of flight and fancy
Because I've made off now
And all that's left of
What I used to be
Is sung softly in the lullabies
That help you fall asleep

Dream Girl

Bloom

Nashé

I would only like
To lastly tell you
That I'm not mad
At you for the fact
That acting
Above love
Was the only
Act of self
Preservation you knew
What strife
It must stir
To crave love
So badly and also
Be so deathly afraid
Of what that love
Leaves you open to
I know there is
No closure
For something like that

For You

And even so
There's nothing I regret about loving you
I know it was something that you needed

Always

when you ask
if i write about you
I want to tell you yes
And no
You embody so many things
To me
but this is not the first time
i've felt
you see
the poem is like a house
Our memories welcomed guests
Always greeted with open arms
At the door
We laugh bountifully together
but these walls
have hosted stories just like
This before
Yours is not
The only figure
to have roamed
these halls

For when you ask

The loneliest thing
To realize as a poet
Is some people
Will be things you
love so that they set
your heart on fire
with the need to write
About them
only to be just poems
Years from now

Just Poems

There are some people
Who have a dark so dazzling
That you can't help but
Jumping in
Without a care
For if you drown or not

dark

You'll know breath
After this pain
And a plethora of days after this rain
Your spine will straighten once more
You've stepped out of the downpour
There is magic

to be had

II

I hold my friends like love letters in my
most trusted journal. Bound together and
nestled tightly with secrets that won't
even dare be whispered.

Between the lines

Bloom

I am grateful
You have allowed me to see
Your soft and sweet
Because out in the world
I've witnessed you bare your teeth
I know that some days
You feel just like me
Like all it would take to knock you over
Is just a breeze
But I know the opposite friend
Have seen the way that you can
Make the world bend
Quiet
There is a power
In your silence
That make weak men tremble
You beautiful
Untamable masterpiece
I pray for your sleep
And your eased worry
You
A woman of plans
And no hurry
What grace you bring
And life you keep
Thank you for showing me
Your deep
It is dazzling

After Angie

Nashé

Boundaries are simply
The outlines which define
You
And the ways in which
You must be
Held and kept

Boundaries

Wrath can be divine

Blessed be those
Who spit their anger
Out so as to
Not burn their
Own mouths
In the name
Of keeping peace
Outside of themselves

Confrontational

I would spend
The rest of my life
Trying to count the stars
I've spent
On wishing you well

Well Wishing

Bloom

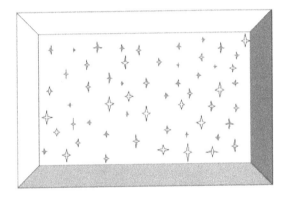

Nashé

when was the last time
That you experienced
Child like euphoria
in which you
Love something so much
That you'd like to do
That thing
Over and over
Until you're bursting
With laughter
And your lungs are
All out of breath
What giddy and glee
It all is

At play

I find that the warmest of women are
Nestled in prayer
And most often
Have a bag of things
They do not know
How to unburden themselves of
But these women
Are the most worthy
Of a clean slate
Of not forgetting
Their past
But forgiving the misdeeds
Of those who were
Less God than them
Only to further their purpose
They are kindred spirits
Of kindness itself
And while they can be
The remedy
It is more suitable
That they rest easy
After all they have seen

The Remedy, after Destiny

Twenty one feels like
Leave your shoes at the door
And come bearing gifts
Or Good news
Feels like
Consider me
And partake in soft tones
When addressing me
If you must leave
Do so quietly
So as to not disturb the flow of things
I think I'm getting into
The flow of things
There is a beauty
In stepping so confidently
Into the unsure
Twenty one does feel unsure
But it does feel loved
And wanted
Pursued if nothing else
Worthy of pursuit
And twenty one definitely
Knows what's good for me

TWENTY ONE

This is an ode to the girls
Whose mothers are no longer
Enamored with them
Girls that have watched
The adoration and romance
Fade
Girls who need to know
It is okay
To still pick up
When softness calls
Because
It does not belong to her
The generational curses
that they swallow
Were never their burdens either
they need not apologize
For the way they carry
A weight
they should rest knowing
they are the beginning
Of the most beautiful end
their bloodline has ever seen
For the girls who are no longer
Everything for everyone
they are not
nothings
It is okay to be
breath and bone
Quiet moments
left alone
Soft girl
Beautiful woman

Nashé

So capable of grace
That she was never shown

An Ode to Daughters

Bloom

I tell my friends often
And with certain joy
That we have become
Those aunties
The ones
That would shine
When we looked at them
She look like sweet
Look like butterflies
And enough candy
To rot your teeth
The auntie I am
So inspires the niece
I used to be

Auntie

I believe God is an artist
In the way that everything about life breathes
The poetic nature of all of the natural
The way the trees
Stretch towards the underside
Of a caressing breeze
It must be so
That God painted
Each of the clouds into the sky
Singularly a spectacle
Of unique brush strokes
God's love
Residing in each and every work
As they are all apart of Her
God giving each of these creations
The desire to create
A passion that lives
In each part of life and death
And experience
How an artists heart may feel everything
And still return home

Creation

The dust returns to the ground it came from and the spirit
returns to God who gave it

You see
We return to the love
We are made from
And we rejoice
To look to the sky
And see the very dust
We came from
Looking back at us
What dazzling comfort
To have been
And continue to be
To love fully
And live on
To grow roots
And plant memories
To watch your life
Grow as the seasons change
And learn to grieve as
All things both go and stay
To be of the earth
And celestial
To value life
And love it well
We are made of
the love we came from
And so one day
We shall return
The memories of his love
Will never fade

Nashé

They grow even stronger
With each passing day

For Chris

Some nights the drive home
Can feel like 100,000 miles
But I want you to know
That your moon and mine
Are still the same
When you close one eye
They are both still
Just the size of the tip of your thumb
when you hold it up to the sky
You're not too far
To hear me whisper you well wishes
There has always been
A boldness in the way
Your kindness is honest
The way you have built the everlasting
Garden at home
That need not to be watered
Or tended
Only visited by those who love you
I go there often
At night
Just to hold my thumb up to the sky
And see all that you have grown here
The drive is long
But here
Our moons are still the same
And your love whispers softly
Through these overgrown leaves
That are still reaching towards you
I know you aren't too far

Still Grows, after Taylor

I love you like deep deep breaths
Love you like relief
and real good sleep
love you with every single
Heart beat
Love like I know
This will always taste sweet
At least to me
With you I can just
Let things be
I can dream big
Without a single expectation
Hanging over me
Just allowed to breathe
And be
Something of yours
Both treasured and free

Effortlessly

There is wrath
In every divine being
Both Gods old and new
Reign down on those
Bold enough
To cross the line
Cross a boundary
Your wrath is divine
When you defend your
Boundaries
There are those
Who would erase
The lines that keep
And hold you
If only to squeeze
You as tightly
As it pleases them
To drain you dry
As this eases them
Show your anger is purposeful
So there will be no doubt

Deity

ever grateful
for the anger
that sprouts
when these
boundaries
that hold me
are crossed
what vigor
it is to know
that no love
is bigger
than the
space I
must hold
For myself

Kept

The framework in which
I think of old friends
Is as follows
I do not know them
I have accepted that
None of us will be untouched
By the constance of change
I knew them once
Moreover
I knew them before
A perfect
Freeze frame in time
A mosaic
Of love we knew
And the pain behind
That stained glass
Our lives goes on
And what I knew
of them
Stays here
Undisturbed by the world
And unmoved
By the moments that
Have inevitably passed
By you and I

Museum

Love so deep
It's worn paths well
I don't wish to go
Any further than
You would follow

Follow

There is life and death in
This tongue
In words
We create and destroy
And here I choose to honor
You
This anomaly
Singularly unique
This reassurance of being
A confirmation that this all
Is indeed worth it
How lucky have I been
To have known you
A woman of ideal and intelligence
Please continue on
There is life in you
That has yet to be shared

Value In, after Sasha

Nashé

There are times when
My heart yearns for yesterdays
And while frustrations sprout
I cannot let them grow roots
I quietly hush her
Wipe the tears away
And remember
Tell her this is a truth of being
Somehow along the way
We will lose folks
That she has made room for
Inside the walls of what I once
Believed to be paper mache
I assure her
This is not the end of it all
And though I wish she would
Take precaution
My heart does as she knows best
She keeps on loving fully
And with her all
Even while it hurts us often
The beauty in it all
Makes me believe her
When she says that this kindness
Is worth what happens

After the Fall

As I swept my gaze across the sky
I didn't count
All of the stars
But one
You
Weren't simply born
But burned brightly
Into existence
Made from the ashes
Of what once was destroyed
And I know that's where
Your magic comes from
Being something that
Was believed to be no more
Only to prove
That life still grows here
And that
You can still lead people home

after, Estrello

I wish you soft
Wish you open
And peace
Wish you good nights of sleep
I've watched the light flicker
And also saw it fill whole rooms
I wish you feel home soon
Pray your nights feel light
And your mornings all warm
Your well being be satisfied
I hope you take the time to set aside
Moments for taking in all that's around you
You smell the roses and let music resound
I hope you find pride in all you could do
Having found what joy you may
Even in times of darkness and disarray
You have made this trip before
I pray you find more open doors
When the moon pulls the tides
Far past shores
Hope you remember
That you have always been
The light that guides the way home
I wish your life full
And you never feel alone
During this

Trip Around the Sun

Bloom

I love you confetti
I guess I mean to say
I love you out loud
In color
And all over the place
I love you for all the small pieces
And during your greatest achievements
Love you big
And bright
In all your shine

Confetti

Nashé

You are the most wonderful of things
Music to my ears
These melodies
I'll remember these
To know such joy
And express such pain
You are the soothing notes
After the rain
I ain't never known
No love that feels like
Music
But what a blessing
It be
To know you
Both honest
And God sent
Your love be like
Breath and bread
And food and water
How you keep the world
Sustained
I see you balancing
That and your pain
My dear friend
Please know I live to see
Your melodies
On every single tomorrow

See your music, After Roze

Have you seen the way
The sky lights up
When lightning strikes
The way it brings
Brightness to the night
In these moments
Experience the static running up
Your legs
Just past the witching hour
Feeling thunder
Boom through a room
Can give you the same sensation
As standing in front of an ocean
To be reminded that you are small
And apart of something
Much larger than anything
Your mother's have dreamt of
Before you
Could even conceive of
Still being susceptible to the nights call
When the moon is full
And the rain won't stop calling
You
To step out into the holy spray
That this pink hue is calling
To all the
people
That
Have yet to realize
You've been up all night
Long since the sun has tried
To slip past you
While you were wrapped up
In the magic
Of yet another

Nashé

Full moon
Sweet dreams

Time stamp: 3:22 am

You feel like night time
And long goodbyes
Like I don't want
To go home just yet
Feel like pressed flower memories
And so hard to forget
Like good music
Like maybe I would
Be ready to come home
If it was you
Some nights you feel
Like home too
At the very least
You the song in my headphones
That gets me there safe
All cool air
And fresh escape

Like Home

Nashé

You have waded through
These waters for so many years
I know there have been many
A days that you have wondered
If you will
See land soon
And what a gift it has been
To watch such a treasure wash up
On the shores
Both beauty
And so unsure
I have seen the manners in which
You still experience the feel
Of waves crashing over you
Breathe
You have endured this drowning
But no longer
You are safe here
My love
Be dry
And warm
And home
The trek may be long
But I am here to tell you
That we've
Made it to land

you a La

Here the flowers grow up the walls
And it's always warm
What a way to live
A way to be loved
You can call this feeling
Home
or euphoria
But know that
This is sacred
And this what taught
Me not to be
Afraid
You are
what taught me
not to be afraid
How could I
Have witnessed
Someone so eternal
Something so vast
And ever
Be afraid again
Here I am safe
And warm
And there are flowers growing up the walls
So I'll wait here
For there is
a day when
I will see you once more

Safe, After Olivia

P.S.
There are things
I haven't said
Wind chimes of things
That hang over my head
And make noise when
The breeze blows through here
And there are days
When I light fires
In paper lanterns
And let the things
I've held
So closely to me
Float away

Unsaid

I have such an
 immense love for
The girls that have
Not endured
The things they
Were called
Instead
They ripped the labels away
And wrote their own
These soft beings
Know very well
These bodies are

Their home

Nashé

This morning does feel
Like a resurrection
Of things
A rising of dreams
That we once believed to be
Dead by all means

To Rise

Some friends
Are just the kind of love
That says
I'm on my way
A comfort
soft enough to
Lay your weary head on
For a while
If you ever need
A hand
That holds yours
And still shows you the way

Rest, after Cheyenne

No more of this
Waiting to grow
We clip dead leaves
And move higher
Towards the stars we came from
Allow your roots
To remind you
That they must be
The thing only that holds you
To this earth

Purge

There is nothing else
That cures my ailments
No remedy I've known
That continues to walk me home
Even on cold nights
I want to give you
Every possible flowery nothing
Friend
A companion beyond ages
I know I have known you
Though it may not have been us
We have walked together before
And what joy it is
To walk with you once more

Moonlit walk, After Tewina

I wanna dive
head first into
the night sky
Want the infinite
To cradle me close
And cold
I'd like to meet
the northern lights
Under them I'd gladly
Spend my days
Until I turned blue

Northern Lights

III

Love finds you in the deepest of depths
It will swoop you up
With the quickest of grasps
From the darkest of despair
It will cradle you closely
And keep you steadfast
I pray nothing hinders its path
On its way to you

Godspeed

What is love?
Some days it's just the winding road home
After a night of music
Sometimes it's small enough
To stuff in the bottom of your bag
Because you need it there
To have it close enough to carry on your shoulder
There are nights
When love will wrap its arms around you
Holds you warm and close
And times when it feels
A millions miles away
But allow me to assure you
Love will show up on your doorstep
Unannounced
Bearing no gifts
Only a soft whisper
That writes itself on the fog
Of your glass screen door
"I am for you, and you alone"

Not a single one
Of our bellies will be
Full on the fumes
of a half baked love
so let's make meals together

Home cooked

Nashé

I have had
To conjure the valor
It takes to be
Slow to anger
This life
Didn't hand me gentle
I was forced
To plant and water
It on my own
To reshape this battlefield
Into a garden
Hardy enough
To sustain
This new growth and healing

Valor

You
At the most tender
Of ages
Are waiting for you
On the other side
Of all the water
You refuse to allow
Yourself
Drink fully
Cry freely
You are making
A desert of yourself
And though you may
Survive this drought
A younger you
Will be left thirsty
And unmet
Haven't you realized
This is what
You deserve yet?

Cry

Kids be the most
Triggering of all things
And here I am
Pulling from a bucket
Of love and patience
That I had to fetch myself
The affection can be
On tap for the babies
But there's no way
For me to shut the drain
And let the tub fill
And overflow
I missed the training sessions
On not pretending
When you must be
All the softness
You had to search for
I breathe shallowly
Scared to startle love
And it never find me
There is envy
And healing in it all
My love may be
Back breaking patch work
But I give it freely
For those that come after me
Most days
Are not so gentle reminders
That they
Are not more deserving
Than I was
But do

Deserve more than I got

Overflow

Please don't thank me
for loving you honestly
this is the true tenderness
you always deserved

Yours Truly

I just want
To sit in the rain
With you
All I crave is
To dance slowly in the downpour
I won't mind the way
My clothes stick to me
As long as I can cling to you
And we can dance slow
I could be here all night
Under the cloudy sky
That hides our stars

Dancing in the Rain

My mama
Is a sweep you up
Whirl you around
And set you down rightly
Kind of force
Always smells
Of perfume and cigarette
Smoke
And you ought to
Listen when
She's talking to you
Because she is
No joke
Stern loving
The word "babe"
Passes lips
As easy as
Chapstick
Don't fret none
You are welcome
To confide
Anytime
She is an open ear
And a bigger heart
As far as wit goes
Anyone could tell you
She's smart
My mama be
A roadmap back
To faith
When you are
Lost and weary
We have fought

Rough seas
But even
In the eye
Of a storm
My mama
See clearly
She always has been
A rock you to sleep
Kind of love
And in this life
I'm sure she's given

Enough

I would sell stars
To the night sky
If only to shrink this
Distance
Between you and I
Just to
Capture the serenity
It would give me
To lay lips
On your heartbeat

Distance

Grandaddy called me
On February 14th
A deep and raspy
Happy birthday baby
Curled around me like
warm cigar smoke
8 days late
I know the honor in this
I am not the woman he meant to call
Though I am happy
To be who he thought of
When his late wife
Whispered a reminder
Of the day she was born
Maybe this is him seeing me
Or seeing her
But all I see is ease
I can only pray to be
A woman worth reminding
Folks of her

Belated Birthday, after

Grandma. Betty

Sometimes when I'm with you
I run my finger down your side
To count your ribs
Because I heard
An old story once
About a man's other half
Being made from his
Very own ribs
And most days I'm sure
That I was made
Just for you

Eve

She is soft
And so sweet
She never grits her teeth
She does not want
But simply calls her desires
Directly to her door
She is not afraid of her surface
And will show you so much more
I must protect this
The undying love
She carries
And refuses to put down
Is my sole responsibility
She must be able to cry in peace
Not a single thing should stop her
From sleep
There may be a war raging
But serenity is simply a must for me
For her

Yin

With you
I haven't ever felt
Like I was falling
More so
I have walked softly
Into the warm embrace
Of this love
You so valiantly offer
There was no
Long journey
In search of this
No trial to face
You just showed up
With offering and
Consideration in hand

LANDING

Nashé

I would sing
Ths stars and the moon
To sleep
If it meant that
You and me
Could be as alone
Together as we could be
I would lull
The whole night to
Blissful peace
Just for you and me

To be together

109

I've found myself in a
Take your word for it
Kind of love
It is soft
And giving
It whispers
That there is no need
To explain anything
It says
I already know
And for what it's worth
I still see you
For all the love I've had for you

Whispers

Nashé

If I could
I would
Live in your skin
I would make
The canyon in your back
Where your spine rests
My place of refuge
My food of choice
Would be the blessing
 Of your existence
Just so I could
Have a taste of
A sweet day with you
When I'm without you

Closer

Father I'm so tired
Of asking for forgiveness
Just living with
The hopes
That you love me
Like I love her

Unconditional

Nashé

The star lit night sky
and I have been long time friends
The stars remain quiet
And though
The horizon is often silent
The dead of night
Makes me feel less lonely
Looking to the darkened sky
Fills me with a nostalgia

Less Lonely

Bloom

If I had to write
You and I
I would then be
Tasked with
The challenge of fitting
Every single word
Of two languages
Into those seven letters
Because
I could not
Turn enough
Of phrases
To describe
Me and you
In tandem
There isn't a sufficient
Enough depth
In the words
That I possess
To tell you
The soul baring
Earth shattering
Things that we
Mean to me

Seven Letters

Nashé

The best life
You'll ever live
Is one in which
Love is all that matters
And anything else
Falls by the wasteside

matters

Bloom

Search as far and as wide
As I may
I know I will never find
Any love that loves
Me like this
An adoration so wide
And deep
A love that lays me down to sleep
This love that prompts such kindness
Bountiful kindred softness
As far as the eye can see
A warmth that lets it all breathe
An unearned thing
Feelings that remind you
Of how the wind can sing
Some days it can make it feel
Like the earth won't move
Unless this love says to

The Deep

Nashé

A blessing it is
To wash in the river
Of your love
Blessed baptism
I beg you
Wash me clean
I'll kneel at your knowing banks
To be bathed
In these cool waters
Make confessionals
Of these cold winds
I have been on
Such a journey
And your Jordan
Is the only sustenance
I've seen for miles
Rinse me
And wring me out
Cleanse me
Once more
Shower my sins away

Baptism

For this love
I do not wish
To be forgiven
If this is displeasing
To God
I would simply
Lay my faith at your feet
For you have given
Meaning to words
That were only words
Before
Heaven and hell
Didn't mean a single thing
Till sweet days with you
And long days without you
I have never found you
A conditional savior
My sins add up
To nothing
In the presence of
Such glory
I would
Much rather
Honor this love
What is worship
Next to this
Holy salvation

My Soul to Keep

You take these dull
And broken pieces of me
To hold them closely
Polishing them
Until they shine
Like I never imagined
Such could do

Shine

If you would grant me such
I would live in your front
Right pocket
Reside in the
Underside of your
Purposeful breath
Make mountains and valleys
Of your neck

RIGHT FRONT POCKET

Nashé

Healing is the consistence
Of releasing
And re-releasing
The things that restrict and burden you
As your life before now
Has been moments
Of repression
And reprieve

Cycles

Though the sear
Of suffering can
Be blinding
I so desperately urge
That you look closer
That you move nearer
Through it there are
Sparkling moments
Of the humanity
That is shown
When community
Must band together
To create a base in which
None of us fall through
This is not a request
To further embrace
That which burdens you
But a simple prayer
That you may
See more clearly
That pressure does
Create diamonds
And we can find the value
That lays just beyond

Prayer for suffering

You planted my love for you
In spring
And watered it
You tended it
Though they called you green
You knew all you needed
Was that growers thumb
And so you did
You watched it grow
And damn did we bloom
In summertime
Winter seems millions of
Miles away
And I knew
As I've always known
That we could weather any storm
All you ever wished for
Was to watch me grow
How couldn't I blossom?
Under such warm and soft light
You love me like sunshine
Mind me gently
And you're always there when it rains

Garden

Nashé

Is it uncomfortable?
Well good
The feeling of
A seed bursting through
Their own skin
May not be a pleasant thing
But growth is
Inevitable and beautiful
It may not be joyous
In the process
But flowers sprout anyway
And spring forth in a beauty
That would otherwise
Be lost
Without the discomfort
Required to

Bloom

Printed in the USA
CPSIA information can be obtained
at www.ICGtesting.com
LVHW041240010923
756940LV00010B/800